AN IRISH WHISTLE BOOK

Complete Instruction Book for learning the Irish Tin (or Penny) Whistle.
Basics, Diagrams, Techniques, with Irish Song Airs and Dance Tunes.
by
Tom Maguire

OSSIAN

Demo CD
Available
Separately
(OSSCD121)

Design and layout by John Loesberg
Cover Picture : St. Patrick's Close, by Walter Osborne (1859-1903)
reproduced by permission of The National Gallery of Ireland.
Special thanks to Geraldine Cotter

Published by
Ossian Publications
14/15 Berners Street, London W1T 3LJ, UK

Exclusive Distributors:
Music Sales Limited
Distribution Centre, Newmarket Road,
Bury St Edmunds, Suffolk IP33 3YB, UK

Music Sales Corporation
257 Park Avenue South, New York, NY10010
United States Of America

Music Sales Pty Limited
20 Resolution Drive, Caringbah, NSW 2229, Australia.

Order No. OMB105
ISBN 978-0-94600-590-1
This book © Copyright 1995, 2003, 2008 Novello & Company Limited,
part of The Music Sales Group.

www.musicsales.com

A CD featuring all the techniques and
tunes from this book is also available:
AN IRISH WHISTLE BOOK DEMO-CD (OSS CD121)

Also available are a companion book and tune-CD with
42 Irish Song-Airs & Dance Tunes:
AN IRISH WHISTLE TUNE BOOK (OMB 106)
AN IRISH WHISTLE TUNE BOOK -TUNE CD (OSS CD 122)

Introduction

The Tin Whistle (or Penny Whistle) has been around for quite a while. Originally it was really only meant to be a cheap little toy for the children of the last century. It would still have been a toy today if it wasn't for the efforts of some traditional Irish musicians who showed that this very basic and portable piece of equipment could be turned into a proper musical instrument. It is very well suited to the playing of traditional tunes from many countries. The basic whistle to go with this beginner's book is a 'D' whistle.

Don't worry, we won't confuse you with too much music theory. But you will find that by following the music, explanations and diagrams you'll be able to play almost instantly. The recording available with this book will enable you to hear what the music should sound like so that you can check back and correct any mistakes.

Have fun !

Tom Maguire

Holding the Whistle

The Diagram shows you how to hold the whistle between your index finger and thumb of the **left** hand. Get a relaxed, but firm grip on the whistle. Place your index finger over the first hole (the one closest to the mouthpiece) and support the whistle with your thumb exactly underneath this position.

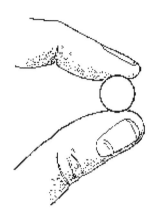

The very first Note

Now blow into the plastic mouthpiece and try to get a nice steady flow of air, resulting in a nice clear sound. Blow just hard enough to overcome the 'Kettle is boiling' sound. Blowing too loud results in ear-piercing noises. Make sure the soft pad underneath your index finger fully closes off the hole.

This next diagram shows what note you've just produced: In music notation it is called the note **B**. The note is exactly on the third line of the **music stave**.

B

To make it easy to remember — below is a diagram showing the whistle with the one hole you covered marked in black (the other holes are simply left open and untouched).

 1

This number is another easy reminder telling you that only **one** hole is closed.

Here are some more notes. For **A** simply add the middle finger of your left hand and with it close off the second hole as well. In the music you see it between the second and third line from the bottom.

A

For **G** add your ring finger of the left hand onto the third hole. Keep on making sure that these notes are crisp and clear when you blow — there should be an obvious step-difference between these three first notes **B**, **A** & **G**. The music shows it on the second line.

G

Slowly, but surely . . .

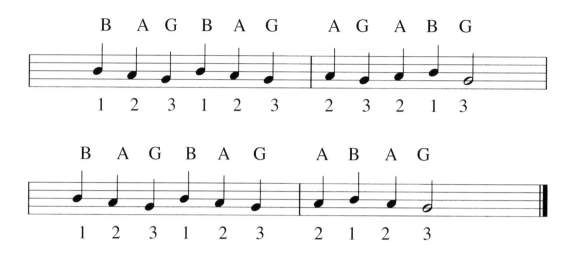

Go over the notes above a good few times — nice and easy — give each note something like a second to last before adding a finger or taking a finger away. Try to make the little exercise (with only three notes, mind you!) sound as musical as you can. Give the two white notes at the end of the second and fourth bars a bit of an extra long blow — make them twice as long as the black notes. Does any of this sound like music yet? Work on this a good few times until you feel confident about the notes, the blowing and fingering.

Tongueing

So far you may have blown each note in little puffs or long breaths to get through the music. This is known as **continuous breathing** and most of the time that's just the right way to play some tunes but sometimes notes are made to sound more separate and distinct. To achieve this, make a **tuh** sound in the mouth by bringing your tongue slightly against the back of your upper teeth. Now try to produce short light bursts of air. This makes for a fairly short, well-defined note. It's called **tongueing**.

Try out our exercise/tune again this time using the new technique — every note is sharply defined now. You could even try the tune using a mixture of **continuous** and **tongued** playing, wherever you feel it's right.

ome more notes now — we'll have to use index, middle and ring fingers of our right hand now as well, so that at the end six fingers will be operating the same six holes all the time. They will be more or less hovering above the holes ready for more action when required.

ext is **F♯** . The ♯ symbol stands for sharp. Don't let this worry you — on the D whistle every **F** is automatically sharp. Bring down the index finger of your right hand on the fourth hole and — this is important ! — add your right hand thumb as well underneath the same position. In the music this note is between the first and second line.

F♯

he next note is **E:** add your middle finger of the right hand on the fifth hole. In the music E is exactly on the bottom line.

E

or the note **D**, cover **all** six holes carefully — seal them off perfectly and try to get a nice soft, full-sounding note. Blow steadily but fairly softly, a shrill sound means you are blowing too hard. In the music D is just below the bottom line.

D

Here are all the notes we've learned so far:

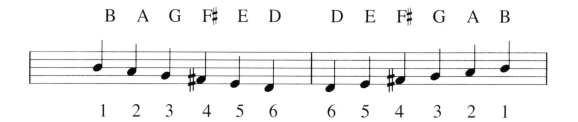

Next — let's try to move up and down the notes several times and especially let's try to remember which is which. Test yourself on the following exercise. Try it with **tongued** and **continuous** blowing.

With a bit of luck all this should sound quite musical by now (if it doesn't — check with the recording and see if you're really playing the right notes). To spin out the above exercise into something like a tune — play the first line twice before finishing with **bars** 3 & 4 (bars are the sections of music between two vertical lines).

a bar

means **repeat** this part from the start, so in the above piece play the first line twice and then play the second line just once.

Even though you may never have played music before, you will recognise quickly how in all tunes and songs you've come across, some notes seem to last longer than others. In the previous exercises you noticed how the white notes lasted twice as long as the others.

Let's have a look now at our very first little song/tune — 'Twinkle, Twinkle' (a tune that has different names in different countries). If you know this air, you will nearly automatically play some notes longer than others. Sing it first and tap your foot along with the beat — nice, steady tapping! As you sing, you will find that most of the words and syllables seem to last one tap except for **Star** and **Are** which really sound longer. It seems that the notes that represent Star and Are last twice as long and ring through two taps.

tap	*tap*	*tap*	*tap*	*tap*	*tap*	*tap*	*tap*
Twin-	kle,	Twin-	kle,	Lit-	tle	Star ——	

tap	*tap*	*tap*	*tap*	*tap*	*tap*	*tap*	*tap*
How	I	won-	der	what	you	are ——	

Once you have grasped this it becomes much easier to understand the different patterns of notes in all kinds of music and also easier to see straightaway which notes have to be kept on longer and which ones only last briefly.

This Black note gets one beat (Technical name **Crotchet**)

This White note gets two beats (a **Minim**)

Now turn to the next page and try 'Twinkle' using all this knowledge. To keep everything steady, tap your foot along at a rate of about a second for each tap.

By the way, as you will notice, most of the tunes chosen for the instruction part of this book are very common and very plain ones that most people are familiar with. This is a very good way to get slowly used to the whistle without having to cope with some Irish tunes that are beautiful, but you've never heard of. We're leaving the real Irish music for the Tune-Section in the back of the book.

TWINKLE TWINKLE LITTLE STAR

Notice how two numbers have appeared behind the 'squiggly' sign (The **Clef**) at the front of the music: the bottom number tells us the basic unit of notes are crotchets. The top number shows how many of these there are in each bar — in this case there are four crotchet notes in each bar basically. Remember, the white notes count for two! Incidentally, note that the second F sharp does not have the sharp sign behind it. All notes of the same name within the same bar are meant to be played sharp. This simply makes the music look less cluttered.

Try 'Twinkle' using ordinary blowing as well as tongueing and see which sounds nicer. You may even combine both techniques. Also try to emphasise certain notes by playing them just a tiny bit louder — this is after all what you do when you sing as well. Try to accentuate every first and third beat in 'Twinkle' and you'll notice the difference!

Rhythm is not the same as speed — the black and white notes only tell us about the length of time these notes last in relation to each other. Of course you could play this tune at 90 miles an hour or you could play it very, very slowly and make it sound like a funeral dirge.

ur second tune helps us even more in understanding the length of the notes. **Frère Jacques** is also in 4/4 timing; four beats (taps) in a bar. I do hope your French is up to this, use the English version otherwise!

ing it first and notice how at 'Sonnez les Matines' (Morning Bells are ringing) the syllables sounded much quicker compared to the other notes. These are **quavers** and look like the usual black ones but come with a little flag attached to them when they're on their own or else connected together when there's pairs or even larger groups of them.

quavers:

FRÈRE JACQUES

To complete the scale — going from a **low D** note to a higher sounding **D** — we learn two more notes. First **C♯**. This is a bit of a balancing act: there are no fingers to cover any of the holes, keep your thumbs at the usual places and let the fingers hover over their holes. Don't move those fingers away too high, you'll need to get them down again soon! In the music C♯ is between the third and fourth line.

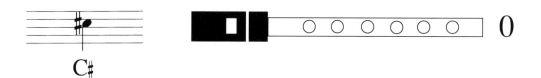

C♯

We'll finish with another D note, very similar in sound — but sounding more like a high-pitched relative of the D we know already. This is a D note which is a leap higher in pitch — such a leap is known as an **octave**. To get this **high D** cover all the holes except the first one — now blow slightly harder (**overblow**) than you normally would. In the music the high D is on the fourth line.

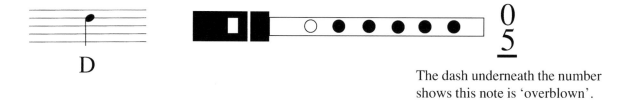

D

The dash underneath the number shows this note is 'overblown'.

Check the steps of your scale now by moving up from **low** to **high D** and make sure that the high D really is a step above C♯. This will take some practice but you will succeed.

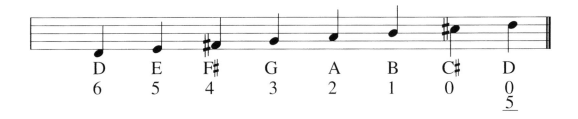

D	E	F♯	G	A	B	C♯	D
6	5	4	3	2	1	0	0
							5

The names of the notes are the first seven letters of the alphabet only, so that after the note G, another A is found. Like our low and high D's, the other notes too have high and low-sounding relatives in other octaves.

The best thing now is to let you 'loose' on a good few nice songs and tunes to try out all your knowledge and techniques. **On Top of Old Smokey** has a 3/4 rhythm — give it a brisk, waltzey pace, tapping **1**, 2, 3, **1**, 2, 3 with three beats between bars. White notes with a dot behind them last for the full three beats. Several times in this song two white notes are tied together across two or more bars (this is called a **Tie**); blow the three counts on the first note shown and continue to blow for another three notes to cover the second one. There is no gap, no new note is sounded.

Notice how, rather than showing each individual sharp as we did before, there are now two sharps fixed at the front of each line just behind the **Clef**. This is in effect the **Key Signature**. From now on whenever you see the Clef followed by two sharp signs it means that *every single* **F** and **C** is a sharp one, until we're told otherwise. Once again this is a music-writing device to make the page look less cluttered with signs and symbols. The two sharps will tell you you're in the key of D and basically all F and C notes are sharp — the way you learned them first.

On Top of Old Smokey

The **Dawning of the Day** is an old march in 4/4 rhythm which also serves as the air to several songs. Watch out for the dotted notes. Apart from the white notes that are dotted we now also have black ones. Hold these notes on half as long as their own value:

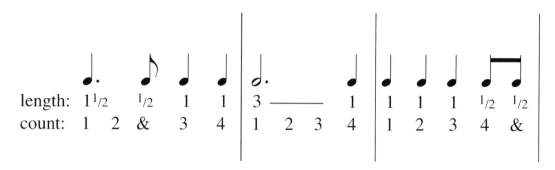

length:	$1\frac{1}{2}$	$\frac{1}{2}$	1	1	3 ———	1	1	1	1	$\frac{1}{2}$	$\frac{1}{2}$
count:	1	2 &	3	4	1 2 3	4	1	2	3	4	&

THE DAWNING OF THE DAY

In the Key of D *all* **F** and **C** notes are sharp — no problem on our D-tuned whistle, as they are already made sharp for us! However, many more tunes may be played by using a second key, the key of **G**. By removing the sharp from our **C♯** and now showing it as plain **C**, or **C♮** (C natural) we can now play even more tunes that happen to be in the **Key of G**.

C♮

Play **C♯** and **C♮** and notice the difference (a half-step really!). The following tune uses precisely the **Key of G** and that **C natural** we just learned. Don't forget to 'naturalize' *every* **C** when you see one ! **In Dublin's Fair City** is in the key of G with only one sharp at the beginning of the piece, indicating that only all the **F**'s are sharp.

IN DUBLIN'S FAIR CITY

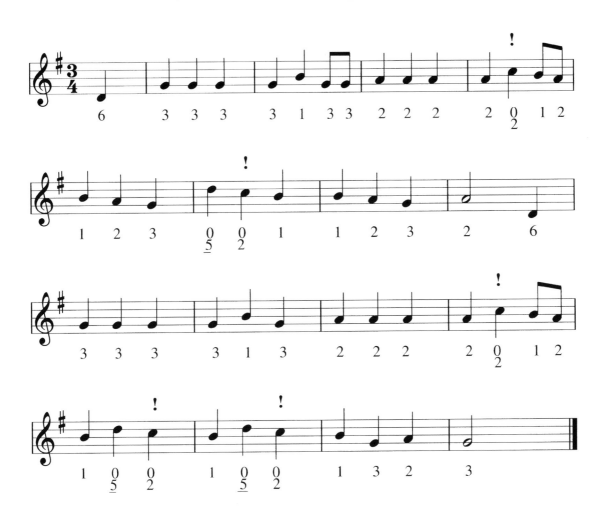

In the next tune **Amazing Grace** we encounter the **triplet**, a small bunch of notes played quickly which only take the time of one single beat altogether.

equals

We know how to produce crisp, separate notes already. Let's now have a go at playing some notes in a smooth, flowing fashion. This is known as **Slurring** (legato officially) and to us it simply means that the flow of air is not interrupted as you change from one note to the next. It is in effect your fingers opening or closing holes that will produce the next note.

a slur

For most traditional tunes such as reels or jigs the bulk of the music tends to be slurred, with the breathing being mainly continuous and the fingers flicking up and down to create the next notes. With the slower tunes it often helps to only slur some notes, tongue the notes that carry stresses in the music, while the rest is played with shorter or longer puffs of breath.

Something looking similar to a slur, but with a completely different function is the **Tie** (Like the ties we used in **On Top of Old Smokey** at page 13). This is used to show that the duration of a note is held on for the length of its value *plus* the length of two or more notes which are 'tied' to it.

tie   slur   slur

ow let's have a go at **Amazing Grace**, which has both ties and slurs in it. Again, go fairly slowly on this old hymn, nicely slur the quavers and hang on to those tied dotted minims.

AMAZING GRACE

Some other Rhythms

6/8 is quite a common rhythm for some songs and especially dance tunes. It consists of a basic 6 quavers in a bar, Usually these six notes are grouped together to show the rhythm:

A dotted quarter note ♩. equals ♪♪♪
A dot behind any note adds half its own length to it.

L eave the whistle aside for a moment and try out the following 6/8 rhythm while tapping at the spots indicated. Tap twice in every bar and say the words.

Ham and eggs and butter and sausages, Ham and coffee and bread with cheese.

A lthough there are really 6 quavers to make up each bar, in reality there should be a sustained two-type feel. Be sure to put some stress on the first and fourth quaver positions.

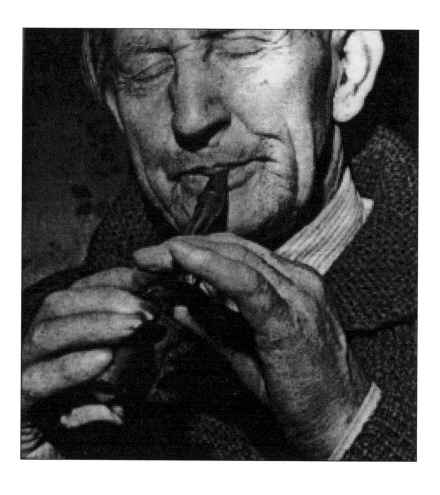

To illustrate a 6/8 rhythm, let's take an actual tune, in this case a nursery rhyme. **Here We Go Gathering Nuts in May** is as old as the hills and known to most. You'll find this exercise useful as you're already familiar with its basic rhythm and it will serve as a guide when learning traditional or other types of tunes.

HERE WE GO GATHERING NUTS IN MAY

Music reading is quite a skill. Many people get dazzled by all the weirdness and complex look of the music notation. If you have been able to follow this book so far, and even if not everything is clear, you have made enormous strides and are very close to having a grasp of the basics of it all.

So far we only really had to deal with a handful of notes (thanks to the simplicity of the whistle as an instrument) and in fact with only a few more additions you will be able to read and play most music that's suitable for whistle. Simply look for tunes written in the **Key of D**, (two ♯'s after the **Clef** at the beginning of a piece) the **Key of G**, (one ♯ after the Clef), and occasionally the **Key of A**, (three ♯'s after the Clef).

Key of D: all F's and   Key of G: all   Key of A: all F's,
C's are sharp   F's are sharp   G's and C's are sharp

With a basic, traditional D-tuned whistle you should be able to play most tunes in these three most commonly used traditional music keys. Eventually you might like to try out whistles in different tunings, so that, while using the same fingering as before, you will produce the scales of those particular keys/tunings.

In any case many traditional musicians will often use a combination of playing by ear (picking up tunes, and memorizing them) and writing and reading simple tunes. Eventually, being able to play a piece after hearing it a few times will become a great asset and this is something most traditional players have in common. The joy on the other hand of browsing through collections of tunes and slowly, but surely trying them out is something just as special.

For those who want to carry on learning the whistle in the traditional Irish style, Ossian Publications have produced *Geraldine Cotter's* TRADITIONAL IRISH TIN WHISTLE TUTOR. This book starts from scratch, showing all the essential techniques and finishes off with a huge tune section with 100 Irish dance tunes.

ere is a summary of the most common rhythms used in folk, pop and other music. Remember that the bottom number indicates the basic unit of beats, while the top one shows how many of these will occur in each bar. (The exceptions to this are often the first and last bars of a tune, as these two will normally be joined together in a repeat).

2/4   2 crotchets in a bar; hornpipes, marches, polkas, reels and breakdowns

3/4   3 crotchets in a bar; slow airs, songs, waltzes

4/4   4 crotchets in a bar; polkas, marches, reels, hornpipes, set dances, old time

6/8   6 quavers (2 beat feel) double jigs, set tunes

9/8   9 quavers (3-beat feel) slip jigs

12/8   12 quavers (4-beat feel) slides, single jigs

or good measure, here is the tricky **G♯**, a note which is likely to show up in tunes set in the key of A. The third hole has to be closed only halfway, which will take a while to master. Once you can do it, it does mean that a great many tunes in three different keys are now open to you.

G♯   2½

ere are some more notes in the higher octaves of notes you've learned already, which will complete your range and will give you access to hundreds of tunes. Remember that all these are to be 'overblown'.

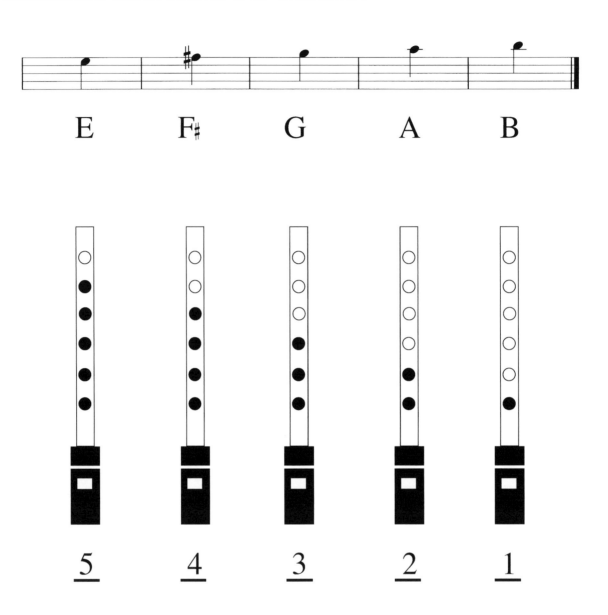

E   F♯   G   A   B

5   4   3   2   1

Our next tune **Morning has Broken** has a straightforward 3/4 rhythm, much like **On Top of Old Smokey**. It also features two **ties**, where the first note is made longer and carries over into the next bar. Simply play the first one and tap for six full beats. Also included in the third bar is a **high E** note (see last page).

MORNING HAS BROKEN

23

Some more Music symbols

stands for four semiquavers equalling in duration one crotchet.

DOTTED quavers: 2 quavers, the first here is dotted to make it last a little longer than the second (it snatches its extra time from the second notes which because of it is only half as long) This is often used in songs, reels and horn-pipes. In some pieces use is made of the so-called 'Scotch snap' in which instead the first note is the quick one.

TRIPLETS: 3 notes played in the time of one crotchet

the NATURAL restores a note to its original pitch: in the case of a C note with this sign play this note and every other C in that bar only as a natural. In the next bar (unless another ♮ appears) all C's are again sharp.

is a REST (no sound) for the same length of a ♪

is a REST (no sound) for the same length of a ♩

is a REST (no sound) for the same length of a 𝅝

PAUSE

back to start and REPEAT

REPEAT this passage

FIRST ENDING, at the repeat skip this bar and continue at 2.

1.

DC (DA CAPO) go back to the very start and play till FINE (end)

D.C.

24

J ust a small recap on the various notes and their duration. The crotchets and quavers are a bit like fractions in maths.

 a crotchet equals two quavers ♪ ♪ or four semiquavers ♫ ♫ the shorter notes are often **beamed** together in written music to make it look neater:

♩ a minim lasts as long as two crotchets ♩ ♩

♩. a dotted minim lasts as long as three crotchets ♩ ♩ ♩

S o much for all the theory — keep up a steady routine of practice, which as we all know makes perfect. Breath control, a general understanding of the music and a minimum of technique will all materialise as you keep on making progress. Listen to recordings and of course live sessions with whistle players.

I n the instruction part of the book so far, we've been using all kinds of tunes. Most of them were well-known popular songs or even nursery rhymes, which is a great way to understand the basics of the notation and the rhythm. The next part of this book will give you hours of pleasure with a selection of some well-known old Irish airs as well as some traditional dance tunes which may be new to you.

S o far, the music you played was made 'easy' for you by providing the name of each note printed underneath it. Many books feature other 'aids' such as endless tablature pictures of tiny whistle-diagrams for each note, or in some cases a system called tonic solfa is put on top of the music. At the end of the day, the real music you'll be facing will be a lot more bare-looking, very much like the last pages of this book. Now that you know all the basics it should be possible to manage reading the music as it is. When in doubt just ask yourself what the name of the note is and where to find it on the whistle.

A second book to match this one is also available:— It's called AN IRISH WHISTLE TUNE BOOK and is crammed with many of the loveliest Irish airs, lively music by O'Carolan and a great selection of Traditional Irish Dance Tunes. A CD containing all the tunes from this book has also been produced.

It's Time to Play the Music !

SPANCIL HILL

Although this tune is in the key of G all C notes happen to be sharp ones — just as if it were in the key of D ! In this particular tune the real and correct name for the key is E minor, but don't let it worry you too much at this stage in your musical career.

Báidín Fheilimí

Play this old song about Phelim and his little boat nice and slowly — feel free to introduce slurs wherever you feel it sounds right.

30

TRIPPING UP THE STAIRS

Break up this Double Jig in small sections- first simply get the notes right by playing slowly.
Only when you're satisfied they're all there try to make them flow smoothly and
only then start to play it faster.

THE SPINNING WHEEL SONG

Nothing terribly difficult here — play a nice steady, waltzey rhythm.

HAYDEN'S FANCY

Play this old Polka in a sprightly manner with a bit of a swing.

SALLY GARDENS

Fairly slow with a lot of feeling, repeat sections in different sequences if you like.
Again, all slurs are optional.

Sí Beag Sí Mor

Six beats to a bar in this beautiful old air written by the blind harper
Turlough O Carolan. Experiment with tongueing and slurring in different places
and mind those very high notes. Slurs are optional.

THE HARVEST HOME

Steadiness is the secret in playing this rollicking old hornpipe.
Practise it very slowly and steadily at first and bit by bit increase the speed until you
reach a tempo of roughly 2 seconds per bar. From start to finish it
should last about 30 - 36 seconds.

SLIEVENAMON

Another slow, waltzey rhythm — look out for the sharp C's in bars 22, 23 & 25.

'TIS PRETTY TO BE IN BALLINDERRY

A gentle, rocking rhythm would fit this old Irish lullaby best.

FOR MORE READING AND LISTENING:

AN IRISH WHISTLE TUNE BOOK, also by Tom Maguire
Ossian OMB106
Accompanying Tune CD: Ossian OSSCD122

TRADITIONAL IRISH TIN WHISTLE TUTOR by Geraldine Cotter
This is a complete method for the Irish Tin Whistle with an appendix of 100 airs and dance tunes. Although suitable for complete beginners, this is an advanced course with particular emphasis on Irish music in all its forms.
Book: Ossian OMB31
Demo CD: OSSCD35
Double CD with all the tunes from the book: OSSCD107

TOTALLY TRADITIONAL TIN WHISTLES
If you ever wondered what can be done with a modest little instrument such as the tin whistle —
here's your chance! 16 tracks by ace players: Willie Clancy, Miko Russell, John Doonan, Fintan Vallely,
Josie Mc Dermott, Michael Tubridy & Cathal McConnell
Ossian OSSCD53

Many of the song airs in this book appear in their complete version with words and guitar chords in :
FOLKSONGS AND BALLADS POPULAR IN IRELAND by John Loesberg
Volumes 1, 2, 3 & 4 (OMB1, OMB2, OMB3, OMB4)

www.musicsales.com